On the other side of the beach, light

Voices of Syrian refugees on war, flight, and a new life

Daniel Skyle

Stairwell Books //

Haunting in their detailed evocation of what it means to live through conflict and leave your home, Daniel Skyle's tender, vivid and redemptive poems give voice to the victims of the war in Syria. Coaxing the sublime from a terrible violence with "a desperate gentleness", this collection will stay with the reader long after the last page has been turned. – **Jack Houston**, author of *The Fabulanarchist Luxury Uprising* (The Emma Press)

These words really describe mine and others stories, emotions, and memories. This is our life; this is how we felt. It is so important and wonderful that people can read these stories. Especially those who have no idea about how refugees have suffered in war, and what their situation was like when they left their country, and the dangers they faced during their journey to Europe. We had no choice. A thousand thank yous for telling the world about the stories and pain of refugees. – **Hanna**, refugee from Syria

On the other side of the beach, light by Daniel Skyle gives voice to the experiences of many Syrian refugees. The poems are strong and sad, brave and tearful, often with hope at their heart. From the woman arriving to safety in Denmark, to the mother remembering kindergarten in Syria, to the guilty soldier, to the Doctor unable to use his healing skills in Europe, they remind us of the reality of pain and suffering war inflicts. Their light shines into many dark places. – **Wendy Pettifer**, Human Rights lawyer in Calais, Athens, and Cairo turned poet. www.lovelines.net

I not just loved them, these poems resonated so deeply and seemed to capture the experience... I found it painful, yet hopeful, and authentic. Each refugee's voice comes through, and I think it's something everybody should read, because I think they don't they get amplified enough. The more we hear those voices, the better we are as a society. And it's so important for those words to be written down, and just be out there in the world. – **Julia Lydien**

Certainly the people of our world need to hear serious and new words in the form of poetry about refugees that come from the depths of the heart, and the best serious and new words that surely sit on the heart are in Daniel's poetry.

Poetry is the common language of all the people of the world, and it is a good poem that best conveys the pain, feelings and problems of refugees to the people of the world.

My name is Mohsen and I have an academic background in horticulture engineering. I come from Afghanistan and I became a refugee in Sweden in 2015. I left my country with my wife and my small daughter. After we arrived in Sweden we faced several problems but fortunately we found many best friends that helped us. – **Mohsen Naderi**, engineer, refugee from Afghanistan

What is it about poetry that makes it the ultimate refuge? Is it its connection to the heart? Or is it something deeper? A better example would be hard to find. – **Red Pine**, translator

Daniel Skyle's *On the other side of the beach, light: Voices of Syrian refugees on war, flight, and a new life*, offers a poignant portrait of the hardship, suffering, and displacement of Syrian refugees and their struggle to survive. And yet, many of the verses that Skyle derived from his interactions while working in Syria and subsequently interviewing refugees in Sweden, brim with hope and an appreciation for their new home.

The simplicity and syntax of Skyle's verses reflect the halting, anguished voices of powerless refugees who, nonetheless, persist, struggling for survival with a muted optimism that salves the scars of their trauma.

The collection of moving poems takes the appreciative reader through an emotional journey full of pathos and loss, yet suffused with muted optimism. Through these spare verses, Skyles has offered a voice to voiceless refugees, and with his empathetic rendering, a chorus that celebrates the power of their resolve. – **Michael O'Neill**, aid worker

Since mankind began to wage war there have been refugees. Our history books are filled with stories of displaced persons and migration waves. Yet these tragedies are all too often reduced to dates and statistics. What we need is an awareness of the reality behind the words – months or years of danger, fear, suffering, despair and hope. On the other side of the beach, light, by Daniel Skyle, is a compassionate attempt to recreate this refugee experience in poems. I recommend the book to anyone interested in the human condition. – **Professor Ingemar Ottosson**

Published by Stairwell Books
9 Carleton St
Greenwich
CT 06830 USA

161 Lowther Street
York, YO31 7LZ   UK

www.stairwellbooks.co.uk
@stairwellbooks

On the other side of the beach, light © 2022 Daniel Skyle and Stairwell Books

All rights reserved. No part of this publication may be reproduced, stored in or introduced into a retrieval system, or transmitted, in any form, or by any means (electronic, mechanical, photocopying, recording, e-book or otherwise) without the prior written permission of the author.

The moral rights of the author has been asserted.

ISBN: 978-1-913432-38-6

Cover image: Daniel Skyle

These poems are dedicated to

Those fleeing war and conflict

The White Helmets

The poets of Syria

and

To my grandmother, the author Brita Skyle (1919-2011)

Table of Contents

Preface	1
Refugee	3
The next symphony	4
The Long Step	5
On the other side of the beach	7
One year later	9
Where is your passport	10
The sky is not yours anymore	11
So big	13
Another language	14
You are a teenager	15
Right, wrong	16
Untitled	18
I'm a specialist	19
The little ones	21
Are you one of them?	23
When we can say the words out loud	24
White helmet	26
Annika and I laughed today	27
"Paper" "Less"	28
Tent canvas stage	29
Going to kindergarten	30
Only reality left	32
Your eyes	33
My soul will sing	34
I want to show my own skin	35
A song of trees	36
War correspondent	37
Grey area	38
I couldn't do anything	39
Set to Global	40
The hidden library of Darayya	41
Writing about horror	43
Accuracy	44
Before the war came, we were human	46
Immigration official	47
They have stolen the sky from us	48

To those who once were kidnapped	49
Michelangelo in Syria	50
The silence of the vanished	51
Internally Displaced Heart (IDH)	53
Play war	55
A little world	56
Damn them	59
Acknowledgements	60

Preface

There are so many people who are voiceless in the world. Their voices have always interested me; their hidden stories, their incredible strength. The poems here come from my work helping Syrians who were fleeing the war in Syria. I have written poetry my whole life, but the more I listened to them, the more I felt I really had to help get their stories heard.

A few of the experiences here are my own, but most come from refugees I have known or who I interviewed for this book. Many are based around the war in Syria; what happened in the war zone (and still is happening), the dangerous flight, sometimes done while holding your child in your arms, and then the journey of integrating in a foreign place as you try to rebuild a shattered life. The destinies in these poems exist in any conflict, in any war, all over the world. If you have refugee neighbours or refugee parents, they probably lived these stories, just rarely talk about them.

I interviewed them, then I wrote poems based on their stories. Those I interviewed were generous with their time. They showed great kindness in sharing some of the worst moments of their life, so that others might understand what war is like, and why refugees flee. We will probably see even more of these experiences the coming decades, as climate refugees leave nations that are destabilising due to global warming.

And in the middle of the darkness of war, there can be the light of a new life. To those who managed to get away from the war and landed in new countries, there is the possibility to start again; somewhere safe for your children to grow up, far away from snipers, torture, and barrel bombs. Some of the poems have voices from this integration and from the humor, hope, and challenges that can come with it. I hope that a freer Syria will rise from the war, and that light and joy will blossom there again.

I have consciously tried to keep the poems simple. I wanted to let the speaker's voice come through rather than my own. I also wanted to keep them simple as I don't want to write poems that make war, torture, and bombed hospitals seem beautiful.

I began writing and doing interviews in 2015, and over the years, as the conflict evolved, I cut some poems and added others, to reflect what was happening. I tried to weave a tapestry that included voices and experiences from all across the conflict.

There are some things you wish you never had to write about, words you simply wish would not exist. Most of these poems move in that part of reality where only reality is left. I have still tried to write about it, since it's such an incredibly important story to tell. Many who live through such times rarely get a chance to have their story heard.

Some of the poems I wrote in the broken fashion of the voice who told me the story, in the rythm of trauma. If there is one thing that poets can do in conflicts and during dictatorships it is perhaps to help give voice to the voiceless. Through this, maybe we can help give back power to those who looked powerless.

During my work and research I have heard stories I never want to hear again. Some so horrible I will not repeat them to anyone else either. Those who know are doomed to knowing. And still I have only been a guest to these stories, I was not forced to live through them.

I have also over and over again heard stories about incredible bravery, never-ending love, and compassion so great it's a miracle that the human heart can even contain it. And for most of the time while writing these poems, I had the priceless luxury of living in a country at peace.

These are the stories from those who didn't, and those who still don't. I hope I can help make their voices heard.

Daniel Skyle, London and Sweden, 2021

Refugee

There is a hole
where my life
used to be

I'm a weave
missing
strands

I'm a puzzle
with pieces
I can't find

I sought refuge
without knowing
I'd become a refugee. ✏

The next symphony

I am only arms
and love
now

I swim
high above the fallen wrecks
my life is on my back

I am a musician
I wanted my life to be song
instead

I swim here
my daughter on my shoulders,
hunting for land

She
is the note
that begins the next symphony. ✎

The Long Step

You take the long step
down onto the platform,
that one step
full of all the longing in the world.

You're young;
a veil around your hair
you just breached the siege
of big men

who guard the border
between Sweden
and the War:
the hands who check ID

at Copenhagen Airport.
So large, so scary;
you still get afraid
despite all that you saw in Syria.

Whisper:
these are the men
who can make a whole journey of suffering
become meaningless.

You remember the screams
after the bombs
more than much else,
hear them, in the small sounds of life:

car engines whining,
bus doors wheezing,
train brakes squealing,
are the screams of friends, neighbours, your

little brother.
But when your foot lands
on the station platform
all the sounds are gone.

You stand there, looking around.
Who knew peace
is so
full of silence? ⁄⁄

On the other side of the beach
To Alan Kurdi and his family

You are so small
only three years old
you, your family
from Syria

the Mediterranean?
Yes, yes,
we came across the water,
your aunt explains

you, your two brothers,
your grandmother
no dad, no mum
someone killed them

somewhere.
Somewhere
is a
big place.

But you are so small.
The photos of Alan Kurdi
echoed across the world
a week ago

I shake your hand in play;
three years old
I can't get rid of the image
of you

dead on the sand
cold,
pale
next to him

an entire beach
where you are all laid out,
all you children who died
crossing the sea.

But you laugh and
grasp my hand again
you live at least,
you live right now.

I wonder what largeness
your life
will become,
here, on the other side of the beach. ⫽

One year later

I meet you one year later! Happy,
out on town, biking in the summer sunlight
your Swedish much better now, you're smiling,
you got your residency permit
and you are in the programs at the employment agency
hoping to get a job soon, soon, you so badly want a job,
paying back to Sweden
for living here, you insist on it.

When I see you bike off
I choke back tears. I remember
that scar you showed me
a year ago;
the big one, a whole fist deep
into your leg

with different depths
and shining scar tissue
only a blowtorch
could do.

And now you're biking off
into the sunlight,
on your way to the job
you so badly want to have.

Where is your passport

Where is your passport
  I don't have a passport
Pff, everybody has a passport
  I don't have a passport
Why don't you have a passport?
  I couldn't get one
What do you mean, you couldn't get one?
You just order one, yes?
  My government didn't hand them out
  Mohammed's brother was
  tortured
  when he insisted
  they broke all his fingers
  I didn't dare insist
  I want to have all my fingers
  I don't have a passport

The sky is not yours anymore

The sky is not yours
anymore:
the helicopter
just keeps hanging there.

It was the day you fled, you,
your mother, two brothers, sister
your father murdered
two years before

your column of refugees is a dust mosaic
heading for the Turkish border
so close
you can taste the freedom on your tongue.

I see you:
spread out on the road, bitter lines
cut every face, and that special fear
that war gives

that cramps the stomach like a closing fist
that steals the legs
that pulls the lungs tight around the heart
that drains saliva to place a stone inside your throat

which you can never swallow.

Simple packing: you walk on foot.
So close
then the helicopters come
attack helicopters

those that computer games
love so much,
because they never see
how they shred a human being who is loved.

Straight towards your column
attack helicopters
hawks against hummingbirds
attack heli –

and you step out in front of your family
arms out, crucified
you stare down the gatling guns, the rockets
breathe in

breathe out
breathe in
before the buzzing guns
kill everyone

then the lead helicopter tilts, nods to itself
as if on a walk in the park,
and turns around
with the other helicopters behind it

and you're alive.
You're putting one foot in front of the other
crossing the border
alive

until you come to Sweden
full of forests, peaceful
traffic, pointless worry
about

buying trendy clothes
and the helicopter is still hanging there
at night
in the day

in the breath
before the buzzing
kills
everyone ⁄⁄

So big

Desert and sea
the smell of flight
now Sweden's National Day
a maypole standing green
in the sunshine
blond people dancing

Life is so big,
so strange. ⁄⁄

Another language

Three languages,
I speak three languages fluently,
Arabic, Persian
English.

"Fucking towelhead"
are just two words
in one language,
did you know that?
I have begun learning
a fourth one now. ✎

You are a teenager

You are a teenager
from Syria
your sister was with you on the trip
the men threatened you with guns
they took her
you don't know where she is
you haven't told anyone
at your foster home now
you are a teenager
but can't find your way back
to being one

they took your sister

you couldn't do anything ⫽

Right, wrong

So much confusion
in this life, so many things
that can go wrong

If you're lucky, you won the lottery:
grew up in peace, big house
school days, calm life

summer holidays,
foreign vacations,
all the stuff you can wish for

maybe just lacking appreciation
of what luxury
really is

or

you wake up one morning
school in ruins
classes

kept in the basement of your apartement building
mum's family
who live the next city over

no-one has heard from them
for a week now
Khaled's brother

disappeared

he went into the old factory
the one you only leave
when you die of natural causes

so scared, all the time, so scared

dad says
we're fleeing now, across a sea
to safety

they have whole schools there

I want to become a doctor
when I grow up
to stop people dying

we are fleeing now

So much confusion
in this life, so many things

that can go right ⁂

Untitled

Nerve gas
are words
that should never be in poems

or anywhere else.

Words
we can remove
from all dictionaries

so that they wake up again,
the pale, the trembling,
the gasping and the dead.

Nerve gas
should become words
empty of meaning

filled with earth instead,
planted with
flowers

like the used tear gas grenades
in the colony lots
of Palestine.

I'm a specialist

My knowledge is vanishing.
I'm bleeding to death
from a single wound,
the only wound I cannot heal.

I get no help
to get my job as doctor back faster;
asking, asking and asking
my mouth has lost its tongue

– validating my degree?
So much paperwork,
so much doubt
if I ever get my licence back

I had nine years of training
five years of work
at my hospital in Syria,
I – before my hospital died.

Someone steals
my knowledge when I sleep.
Every day,
the thieves come

they steal facts
I dedicated my entire life to learn.
If I'm not allowed to work soon,
all that I have learned

all that I have learned

will be out of date.
The only thing I want to do
is help patients
again.

The only thing I want to do
is start showing my gratitude,
start contributing
to this country.

I'm bleeding
to death. I watch
the bandage poppy blossom,
feel my blood pressure drop

when I look in the mirror
the lips will be blue, cyanosis setting in,
my skin cold and clammy to touch,
my eyes unfocused

I can heal everything
except my own wound
I only want to

help patients ✎

The little ones

We are the little ones
the red-clad soldiers came
with their shields,
cut our village apart
with their whistles,
killed so many
enslaved all the rest
us Celtoi, why can't our village
be left alone?
Why?
We are just the little ones
we don't disturb anyone

We are the little ones
the knights from the West
obey a crazy old man
who says Jerusalem should be saved in the year 1098
– from us?
They invade our town, call it "Marre"
why
it's called
مَعَرَّة النُّعْمَان
Maarrat al-Nu'man
little ones, we are just the little ones
they kill so many in my neighbourhood
slaughter us like lambs
I had a store
my wife is dead
my son, murdered
by the Europeans
why
we are just the little ones

Thiepval
the Germans came
then the English artillery

We had our farm
along the *Route de Pozières*
cows, such nice cows you ever saw
all the old trees gone
my husband disappeared
I am here, with the others who ran
I hear that Thiepval is flattened now
tout est détruit
we are the little ones
we are those who have fled ▰

Are you one of them?

Are you one of them?
Are you one of the volunteers?
Are you one of those
who took a step forward
to help out?
Are you?
Are you one of those
who took the step out
from luxury and peace
and took someone by the hand?
Are you one of them?
One of the volunteers?
Are you one of those
who heard
so many stories of war and pain
that you feel them spilling
past the lid when you lie there, in the dark?
Are you?
Are you one of the them? ◢

When we can say the words out loud

There are poems a poet never want to write
words you never want to say
because they hurt your throat too much

some stories are a virus
once you listen
you carry the infection forever

maybe Homer could
but I can't
write about the shade of pale

in those taking
their last breath
of nerve gas

the Chinese poet Du Fu
lived a life
full of civil war 13 centuries ago

and he understood Hospital 601:
evil is an old lacquer
painted across our eyes.

I don't want to write
about that, I don't
it's night now

I have enough stories
that fill my darkness
that stand by my bed

maybe we can have
another day
to talk about our stories,

to heal, to first whisper the words
then say them out loud
so that free words fly high into the sky

fill with light
letting us
become lighter

and lighter ◢

White helmet

A good heart

hands dipped in dust:

a White Helmet. ⟋

Annika and I laughed today

I talked to Annika today,
I haven't laughed so much for a very long time
I brought *fatteh*,
the real, my grandmother's recipe

and Annika made *dawood basha*
(they call them "meatballs" here,
"meatballs")

I haven't talked to many
who live here
it's difficult to find friends
I am so worried

to make a fool of myself,
but today has gone well. Really well
we talked about our beloved husbands
and laughed for a very long time! ✎

"Paper" "Less"

Afraid
all the time
scared
paper
no paper
"paper" "less"
paper-less
illegal

afraid, all the time
afraid
have to keep away
from many places in town
avoid
uniforms
train stations

fear
it becomes your friend
maybe not a good friend
a relative
you have to
meet

I don't want to go home
I want to be alive
but everything here
comes down to
paper
I didn't know
the whole world
can be built

on paper

Tent canvas stage

The world becomes a small place now:
only a square
covered by tent canvas
and sunlight. The sun feels

different here in Greece
than in Syria.
Strange. It's the
same sun

that shines over everyone, isn't it?

But this little world
is so big: my mind fills it
with the theater stage
of all humanity.

Memories and dreams
nightmares and hopes:
I am a reluctant Shakespeare
not all my characters obey me.

I let my village
become alive again;
I see my neighbours drive their dusty car
the blue one, with the red front door on the left hand side

I hear sheep bells clang
as shepherds drive them home at dusk,
and my family. I see my
family

live again,
their faces smile back at me
on this tent canvas stage
of my big little world.

Going to kindergarten

My daughters
are in kindergarten now, finally.
Amina and Ahlam,
my beloved Peaceful and Dream.

We had kindergarten in the basement in Syria.
When they bombed the school
a woman in my building
set up kindergarten

downstairs. Hidden by concrete and dust
with maybe electricity,
lit by living candles.
they played.

Crayons ran out,
there were too many horrors
to draw
but we had toys left

blankets
became secret forts, with adult faces
floating tense
by candle light

above children who even laughed sometimes.
Now I take them to kindergarten
every day. I am learning a new language,
studying hard at home

and they are safe. Safe. I am
so grateful. Beyond words grateful.
Sometimes
I have bad dreams

about us walking down those stairs
to the basement, their little hands
holding mine so hard
when we hear the first bombs explode

I am heading back down again
to that school in the basement
then I wake up.
We will go to kindergarten tomorrow! ∥

Only reality left

The city's kind sun-shadows
have shrunk: the bomb planes are eating my city
like jackals.

Water and salt:
never before
have I understood how important they are.

There are those
who try to kill their own citizens:
I feel like a beaten child.

Love is seen
in small acts, now:
it is like grains of sand in the storm.

I know I have a voice:
I just don't know
where it is.

I have stopped running, I have stopped bowing:
if the snipers want my suffering
they are welcome to it.

I don't want to make the nomad choice:
my life or my skeleton
stays here.

Your eyes

It is your eyes
filled with love

that I remember
throughout this entire war. ✎

My soul will sing

The Revolution let me raise my voice

finally my soul could sing

In the local jail I lost my trust in those who ruled

I lost my skin in Branch 215

I lost my blood in Branch 248

I lost my mind in Hospital 601

and I lost my bones inside Sednaya

Still I have my soul

Still I am here

Still my soul will sing ⁄⁄

I want to show my own skin

What do you do
kill or die?
What do you do?
Their uniform
burns my skin
Their words
are stones in my mouth
I see things done
that make ash fill up my heart
put our uniform on
or lose your life
I'm too scared
What do you do?
When they say shoot
I shoot to miss
When I can let someone go past
I look the other way
When I can whisper knowledge
I give it like a blessing
I pray that God
will see my real skin
What do you do
kill or die?
I love my people
I love them
but I'm too afraid to die
I want to show my own skin again ⁄⁄

A song of trees

I've heard about forests,
I've heard about trees,
I know seeds grow strong
to reach for the sun

As I leave in the morning
I carry a pen
I draw flowers and trees
on pavements and walls

Because I've heard about forests,
I've heard about trees,
I know seeds grow strong
to reach for the sun

War correspondent

I'm a war correspondent
I live with ghosts and stories
no-one in the First World really cares about

I live to ask questions;
to give voice to the voiceless,
to tell *truth* to *power*

and you know what it's like, in real life?
I fill my hands with gold
from ancient, ruined Palmyra

and watch people sneer
as if I am holding up
apartment dust.

Grey area

I'm a police officer.
They only see the uniform
they don't understand
it's wrapped around a heart

I don't want to deport
refugees
my parents fled here,
from Lebanon

but we get orders
have to follow laws
it's the job.
I just want to help

people, protect
against the bad guys
but why
is everything such a grey area?

What if I could just help those
who are nice
but
everything is such a grey area

I am a police officer.
They only see the uniform
they don't understand,
it's wrapped around a heart ⁄⁄

I couldn't do anything

I couldn't do anything
do you understand what that's like?
I could only watch
I couldn't do anything
I had to
"Morally Based Posttraumatic Stress Disorder"
the doctor says
do something
I still hear them,
I hear the screams
it becomes better with time
do something!
he says
I couldn't do anything
It becomes better with time,
he says,
I couldn't ⁄⁄

Set to Global

Some days the internet in the city
works again,
I post what's left of my life
on Facebook

The readers, don't they understand
I am doing it from inside Syria?
I live in the war zone
why is no-one helping us?

I put up posts
without cats, no photos of the lunch I didn't have
on my Facebook are only posts
about how we are dying

Don't they see them? It's set
to Global
don't they understand?
I don't want any likes

please

just come save us

it's set to Global ⚐

The hidden library of Darayya
To the group of friends who created the wartime library of Darayya in Syria

When they burned
the great Library of Alexandria

you moved the books
into your own.

You caught them, fed them,
read them, spread them

lit a candle
and lit the souls who saw the flame.

Darayya is empty now
sacked by Ceasar's troops

but in my mind
I see the books

flap their pages
stiffly, at first

then fly off the shelves
soar up the stairs

to finally fly free
into a blue and sunlit sky

and later, roost among ruins,
perch in abandoned houses

flocks of books
breeding, cooing

waiting
for their owners to come back

and read again. ∥

Writing about horror

Writing poems about horror
as if arranging flowers
for a flower show

I refuse.

Sometimes
all that is left
is reality. ⁄⁄

Accuracy

War
steals
accuracy.

I used to be accurate before.
Ordered, impeccable, my wife
used to call me "pedantic"

often with some precision.

I was an accountant
at a company, then
after eleven years, at the university.

War, I now
know, steals
accuracy.

It has tried to take my exactitude:
ruins are ugly, gruff,
insulting in their attitude.

Streets
with craters in
follow no traffic regulations.

People are murdered
higgledy-piggledy: God
does not allow us to choose a straight final line.

I sit here in my tent
in Greece. Far from everything:
far from my life, from my house

from my murdered family. Far
from the threats of smugglers,
and their fancy websites

their money-hunger
as you talk to them
over messy café tables

for that final negotiation before the sea.
I have placed my pens with exactly
a centimeter

between them. My bed
is correctly aligned with
all four tent pegs

my five books
lie in order of size,
and I walk laps

of precisely 43 minutes
around the camp four times a day
Accuracy is mine. It's *mine*.

The war is trying to steal my accuracy
and I will not
allow it.

Before the war came, we were human

Before the war came, we were human.
Now people see us on TV
"More people have died in Syria today"
it's as if they think
we don't feel it
that we are so used to death
that we don't feel it anymore

We do, we feel it
We see people die
We bleed, grief
unmans us
for each one murdered.
It's as if they think we are not

human
that we don't have hearts
that we don't have a family
as if we are not human
we feel everything, everything.
Before the war came

we were human ⁄⁄

Immigration official

This person needs
to be extradited
this person has a right to stay, both the mother and the
child
You are from the right country, almost

crystal clear

I make decisions
who lives, who dies
who gets to stay, who gets to go
who should live in limbo, who should keep their hope

I like it.
I hate it.
I am the bouncer
of our country's door

Sometimes everything is clear
we have rules to follow, paragraphs
some should not be here
some are really a danger to us all

Sometimes
more days each week
everything is
never

crystal clear

The parents get to stay, but not the child
I know there is a war there, I *know*
he really is fifteen, not twenty two
I sleep so badly now, I see that

crystal clear ⁄⁄

They have stolen the sky from us

They have stolen the sky from us.
They own it now. I don't look up
to see birds anymore,
just helicopters, fighter planes

flying death.

I have become a connoisseur of jet engines
to find the faintest whisper
of forewarning
about where the bombs will fall.

They have stolen the sky from us.
They are the only ones to have planes:
the rebels
are earthbound

the rest of the world back-bound. No-one
can help
but everyone can ruin things
even more.

They have stolen the sky from us.
I don't look up to see the sun
or to follow
the flight of a bird:

a barrel bomb
lazily kicked out of a helicopter
by a bored soldier's boot
can murder an entire hospital.

They have stolen the sky from us.
But it's only now:
the heavens will become ours again,
the flight of birds

will come *back* ⌁.

To those who once were kidnapped
For Nadia Murad and the Yazidi

ISIS kidnapped you.
Like Nadia said,
made you die again and again

Nails, drawing blood on cheeks
to flee beauty; ash
to hide little girls as boys

Your hell
with laughing
monsters

and
a crisp autumn day in Japan
a master swordmaker far away
leans across his blade

the strongest swords
are beaten against the anvil
again and again

these are the blades
that still protect
after four centuries

Michelangelo in Syria

The master sculptor Michelangelo
once was asked
if he saw the sculpture in his mind
before resting the mason's tool
against the stone.

"No," he said, "I do not create
anything. I look at the stone
a long time first
then see what inside
that needs to be let free."

You fled the war in Syria
and are trying
to understand,
to figure out, analyse, put
into words

standing by the stone
hacking, stabbing, searching
feeling your way, fumbling
at corners,
finding

an angle
that seems to show important news
until the hammer slips,
a piece falls off
revealing

nothing at all.

You stand there, trying to understand
who, what, when, where,
why, how
and hack and hack and hack
to reveal nothing,

nothing at all.

The silence of the vanished

This war
has taught me
many different kinds of silence.

There's the silence
where Ahmed
said goodbye, and I forgot to reply

There's the silence
of a long afternoon at home
when he didn't come back.

There's the silence
of that night,
not wanting to think

There's the silence
of a dawn
that should have stayed away.

There's the silence
of days
that shake their heads

There's the silence
of neighbours
not stating the truth.

There's the silence
where
I can't get air

And there's the silence
of screams,
shared.

There's the silence
of names,
wondering who

There's the silence
of not
telling our son.

There's the terrible
silence
of hope

And there's the silence
where he comes
to hold my hand.

There's the silence
of not
daring to ask

And there's the silence
of grief
controlled.

There's the silence
of my
life

And there's the silence
of a funeral
that never comes.

Then there's the silence
that ends:
we will find the truth. ✍

Internally Displaced Heart (IDH)

I'm going back home now
I'll hang the blue mirror
back in the hall

we just need to buy a new mirror
and build a new
wall.

Mohammed is dead
but maybe he can still lend us a hand,
and smile that happy smile

as we work alongside.
Layla's bedroom needs
rebuilding, of course

and her little bed is gone
but so is she.
My wife Faten is alive

thank God, and my brother,
too. He only has one arm
but together, we'll grow some food.

Men with guns
still walk around,
but I hope

we can have more children
and a peace
to keep them alive.

I'll put up a good hook
by the mosaic
when it's redone, you know,

and hang my white helmet there
near the door
just in case.

My heart
feels internally displaced
I hope I can rebuild it too. ⫽

Play war

I want another childhood
one where we only
get to play
war.

A little world

The hands
have their own life
I just follow
they sniff, turn, search
find
the right stones
– there are people around us, those
who survived the bomb –
help
I cannot scream
only inside
no energy, my voice
doesn't carry anymore
only my hands, they carry
the living, the dead,
those who have not yet made their choice

there, my left hand finds the way
lifts off crushed rock
finds a hole with its nose
a small body, a small
it's a child again
again
so many children
I
children

my hands lift more carefully but
so quickly
in a desperate gentleness
there are people next to me, strong bodies
hearts covered in dust
from bombed lives
a small body
five years old
purple pajamas

– it's night, I have forgotten it's night
somebody has headlights on us –
finally we have her free enough
and my hands lift
with caution empty even of words
so as not to give reality more weight
reality weighs too much already
and
my feet want to run
but can't, my hands
talk sternly to them
holding her little body
against my chest
while my feet want to run
to the hospital
it's close, only two blocks away

they're moving me, hands and feet
together
I cry between them
lobby, overhead lights
a green surgical mask
bloody arms
one of the few surgeons we have left
someone ran ahead
fetched him
she's bleeding
breathing
not breathing, breathing

not
a stretcher, nurses
tubes, a clear mask
with priceless oxygen
to save a little life
they
my hands hold her
no more
it feels like they still do

others hold her now
the stretcher lifts her
from earth

breathing, she's
breathing, she's

breathing, she lives
everybody laughs and cries
and she vanishes
into the culverts
this is where the hospital has moved
a hand with green clothes
holds my shoulder, briefly
the surgeon nods, disappears
she's breathing
I stand there, my hands still
holding her
my feet want to run
for her sake
but she's breathing, she's alive

a little world
survived tonight.

Damn them

Damn them
your skin against mine
in this little room
we breathe together

fitfully
we live
fitfully
we make love

and we refuse to die
damn them and their murdering
damn their hunger
for power

I hear fighter planes
rushing back in over the city
as I sink
into your sky

I want to go so far in
that everything else disappears
that it's only you
and me

in the whole world
damn the murderers
damn their hate
we live

your wonderful eyes
your burning skin against mine
we live
we *refuse* to die

Acknowledgements

To all the refugees who shared their stories, thank you. You were often sharing some of the worst experiences of your life with me, to help other people understand refugees. I felt that was a huge bravery, and a huge kindness. Shoukran ktir. شُكْرًا الْكثِيري.

My deep gratitude to author Bill Porter (also writing as Red Pine) for being such a long-time inspiration, and for being so generous with his time in helping me get this collection published.

Thank you to Lydia Julien, for her lovely phone message book review that was truly humbling.

Thank you again to Professor Ingemar Ottosson, who continued his kind support of my writing for yet another book.

There are several Syrian test readers I would like to thank by name here. They gave great comments, help, and advice, but many still have families inside Syria and are afraid of repercussions from the regime, so I can't name them, and will simply say thank you. Note that names of Syrians giving quotes on the cover have had to be changed for the same reason.

As always, I have had many test readers for this collection, both refugees and others, to make sure I told their stories well. Thank you all for your time and wise words.

And to Ahmed, a Syrian who did me the huge honour of reading this collection in front of me in a café, page by page, commenting on each poem as we went along. I sat there, very nervous, while he showed such kindness and bravery in revisiting his own experience of the war, to help others. Thank you.

Other anthologies and collections available from Stairwell Books

Herdsmenization	Ngozi Olivia Osuoha
Words from a Distance	Ed. Amina Alyal, Judi Sissons
All My Hands Are Now Empty	Linda Baker
Fractured	Shannon O'Neill
Unknown	Anna Rose James, Elizabeth Chadwick Pywell
When We Wake We Think We're Whalers from Eden	Bob Beagrie
Awakening	Richard Harries
Geography Is Irrelevant	Ed. Rose Drew, Amina Alyal, Raef Boylan
Belong	Ed. Verity Glendenning, Stephanie Venn, Amy E Creighton
Starspin	Graehame Barrasford Young
Out of the Dreaming Dark	Mary Callan
A Stray Dog, Following	Greg Quiery
Blue Saxophone	Rosemary Palmeira
Steel Tipped Snowflakes 1	Izzy Rhiannon Jones, Becca Miles, Laura Voivodeship
Where the Hares Are	John Gilham
Something I Need to Tell You	William Thirsk-Gaskill
The Glass King	Gary Allen
The River Was a God	David Lee Morgan
A Thing of Beauty Is a Joy Forever	Don Walls
Gooseberries	Val Horner
Poetry for the Newly Single 40 Something	Maria Stephenson
Northern Lights	Harry Gallagher
Nothing Is Meant to be Broken	Mark Connors
Heading for the Hills	Gillian Byrom-Smith
More Exhibitionism	Ed. Glen Taylor
Rhinoceros	Daniel Richardson
Lodestone	Hannah Stone
Unsettled Accounts	Tony Lucas
Learning to Breathe	John Gilham
New Crops from Old Fields	Ed. Oz Hardwick
The Ordinariness of Parrots	Amina Alyal
Homeless	Ed. Ross Raisin
Sometimes I Fly	Tim Goldthorpe
Somewhere Else	Don Walls
Still Life with Wine and Cheese	Ed. Rose Drew, Alan Gillott
Taking the Long Way Home	Steve Nash

For further information please contact rose@stairwellbooks.com
www.stairwellbooks.co.uk
@stairwellbooks

www.ingramcontent.com/pod-product-compliance
Lightning Source LLC
Chambersburg PA
CBHW051715040426
42446CB00008B/890